Edie Lamb

♫♫ ♪ Can Sing ♫♫
¡en español!

Fun Songs for Learning Spanish

Louise Morgan-Williams & Gaëtane Armbrust
Designed and Illustrated by Jane Launchbury
Edited by Sue Hook
Spanish consultants: Javier Domínguez and Diana Terry
Music arranged by Ed Montgignan

Contents

Published by Passport Books, a division of NTC Publishing Group.
© 1994 by NTC Publishing Group, 4255 West Touhy Avenue, Lincolnwood (Chicago), Illinois 60646-1975 U.S.A.

890 WKT 987654

About This Book

From a very early age, children respond to the rhythms and sounds of the language they hear around them. They have an amazing ability to mimic sounds and to acquire language easily, an ability that diminishes as they grow older.

Action songs and rhymes play an important role in language learning at this early stage. They help stimulate awareness and interest in language, and provide an enjoyable means of playing with sounds and exploring words.

In **I Can Sing _¡en español!_** songs have been carefully selected to appeal to children. The collection includes both original songs that incorporate familiar, everyday themes, and traditional songs loved by generations of children all over the world. On the cassette available with this book, the songs are sung by boys and girls who are native speakers of Spanish.

Each song text is accompanied by a simple music score for children and adults who want to play the songs themselves. The illustrations help children associate the Spanish words with the action and story of the song.

Under each Spanish word illustrated on the vocabulary pages is a pronunciation key to help in saying the word correctly. (There is more help with pronunciation below.) Say the words together, and then see if the child can pick out those words when you listen to the songs on the cassette available with this book. You'll also see the English translation under each vocabulary word. Full English translations of the song texts appear on pages 31 and 32.

As children sing these songs, they will start to become familiar with simple language structures. For example, nouns in Spanish are either masculine or feminine. To help children begin associating the correct gender with the nouns, we have placed a boy or girl symbol beside each of these words illustrated in the book. This will give children a headstart as they move on to the next stage of learning.

We hope children enjoy these first steps _¡en español!_   Louise Morgan Williams   J. Amulund

---

USING THE PRONUNCIATION GUIDE

If you follow the pronunciation guides in the book and listen to the cassette, you will see and hear how the Spanish words should sound. Some of the sounds call for special explanation, however:

_r_   is slightly trilled with the tip of the tongue,
e.g., **bailar, verde, doctor**

_rr_   is trilled a little more than a single "r,"
e.g., **tierra, acurrucaditos**

_h_   is a little more forceful than "h" in English,
e.g., **debajo, roja, jabón**

An underlined syllable is stressed more than other syllables.

In Spain, the letters _z_ and _c_ are usually pronounced like "th" when they are followed by the letters _e_ or _i_. You may notice that pronunciation on the cassettes. In the rest of the Spanish-speaking world, however, these letter combinations are pronounced like "s." For simplicity's sake, the latter is the only pronunciation we present in the book.

Las Cosas Que Me Gustan

Me gusta la tarta,
Me gusta el café,
Pero más me gustan
Los ojos de usted.

Me gusta la fruta,
Me gusta el té,
Pero más me gustan
Los ojos de usted.

Me gusta el pan,
Me gusta la leche,
Pero más me gustan
Los ojos de usted.

cosas †
coh-sahss
things

que me gustan
keh meh goos-tahn
that I like

tarta ♀
tar-tah
cake

café †
cah-feh
coffee

ojos †
oh-hohss
eyes

fruta †
froo-tah
fruit

pan †
pahn
bread

té †
teh
tea

leche †
leh-cheh
milk

3

Los Pollitos

pollitos †
poh-yee-tohss
little chicks

Los pollitos dicen
Pío, pío, pío,
Cuando tienen hambre,
Cuando tienen frío.

Pío, pío, pío, etc.

La gallina busca
El maíz y el trigo
Y les da comida
Y después al nido.

Pío, pío, pío, etc.

Los pollitos duermen
Acurrucaditos
Bajo sus dos alas,
Hasta el otro día.

Pío, pío, pío, etc.

dicen pío
dee-sehn pee-oh
say pio

tienen hambre
tee-eh-nen ahm-breh
are hungry

tienen frío
tee-eh-nen free-oh
are cold

4

maíz †
mah-eess
corn

busca
boos-cah
looks for

gallina †
gah-yee-nah
hen

trigo †
tree-goh
wheat

comida †
coh-mee-dah
food

nido †
nee-doh
nest

duermen
doo-ehr-men
sleep

acurrucaditos
ah-coo-rroo-cah-dee-tohss
huddled up

bajo sus dos alas †
bah-hoh sooss dohss ah-lahss
under her two wings

5

Pinpón

Pinpón es un muñeco
Con cara de cartón.
Se lava la carita
Con agua y con jabón,
Con jabón.

Se peina los cabellos
Con peine de marfil.
Y aunque le den tirones,
No llora ni hace así.

Como siempre obedece
Lo que manda mamá,
Estudia las lecciones
Antes de irse a acostar, acostar.

Y cuando las estrellas
Empiezan a brillar,
Pinpón se va a la cama.
Reza y se echa a soñar, a soñar.

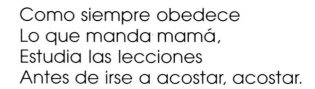

7

Pinpón

Pinpón ✝
Peen-pohn
Pinpon

muñeco ✝
moon-yeh-coh
doll

cara ✝ **de cartón**
cah-rah deh car-tohn
cardboard face

carita ✝
cah-ree-ta
little face

se lava
seh lah-bah
washes

agua ✝
ah-gwah
water

jabón ✝
hah-bohn
soap

se peina
seh peh-nah
combs

cabellos ✝
cah-beh-yoh
hair

peine ✝ **de marfil** ✝
peh-neh deh mar-feel
ivory comb

tirones ✝
tee-roh-nehss
tugs

llora ✝
yoh-rah
cry

obedece
oh-beh-<u>deh</u>-seh
obeys

mamá ✝
mah-<u>mah</u>
mother

estudia
ehs-<u>tood</u>-yah
studies

lecciones ✝
lehc-<u>syoh</u>-nehss
lessons

acostar
ah-cohs-<u>tar</u>
goes to bed

cama ✝
<u>cah</u>-mah
bed

estrellas ✝
ehs-<u>treh</u>-yahss
stars

brillar
bree-<u>yar</u>
shine

soñar
sohn-<u>yar</u>
dream

reza
<u>reh</u>-sah
prays

SÍ MAMÁ

Lecciones 1-5

9

Los Colores Del Arco Iris

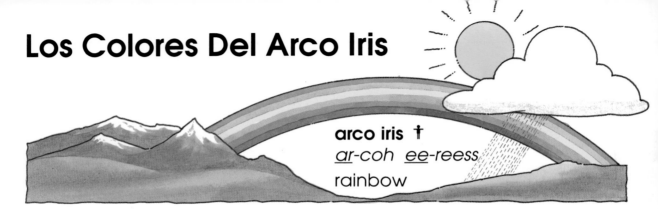

arco iris ✝
_ar_-coh _ee_-reess
rainbow

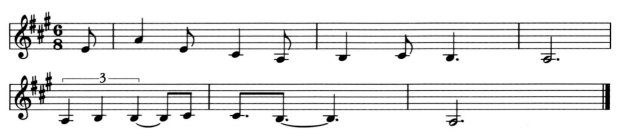

¿De qué color es la manzana?
Es roja, roja, roja.

¿De qué color es la naranja?
Es naranja, naranja, naranja.

¿De qué color es el plátano?
Es amarillo, amarillo, amarillo.

¿De qué color es la pelota?
Es verde, verde, verde.

¿De qué color es el cielo?
Es azul, azul, azul.

¿De qué color es la violeta?
Es violeta, violeta, violeta.

¿De qué color es el arco iris?
Es rojo y naranja, amarillo y
Verde, azul y violeta.

¿De qué color es ...?
deh _keh_ coh-_lor_ ehss
What color is ...?

colores †
coh-lor-ehss
colors

roja
roh-hah
red

naranja †
nah-rahn-hah
orange

manzana †
mahn-sah-nah
apple

verde
behr-deh
green

amarillo
ah-mah-ree-yoh
yellow

plátano †
plah-tah-noh
banana

pelota †
peh-loh-tah
ball

cielo †
see-eh-loh
sky

azul
ah-sool
blue

violeta †
bee-oh-leh-tah
violet

11

¿Quién Llama A La Ventana?

¡Pum! ¡Pum! ¡Pum!
¿Quién llama a la ventana?

Trompetea,
Un elefante grande.

Miau, miau, miau,
Dos gatitos chiquititos.

Beee, beee, beee,
Tres ovejas viejas.

Clo, clo, clo,
Cuatro gallinas blancas.

Zum, zum, zum,
Cinco abejas bobas.

¿Quién Llama A La Ventana?

¿Quién llama ....?
kee-en yah-mah....
Who's tapping?

ventana †
ben-tah-nah
window

1

un
oon
one

elefante †
eh-leh-fahn-teh
elephant

grande
grahn-deh
big

2

dos
dohss
two

gatitos †
gah-tee-tohss
kittens

chiquititos
chee-kee-tee-tohss
very little

3
tres
trehss
three

ovejas †
oh-beh-hahss
sheep

viejas
bee-eh-hahss
old

4
cuatro
cwah-troh
four

gallinas †
gah-yee-nahss
hens

blancas
blahn-cahss
white

5
cinco
seen-coh
five

abejas †
ah-beh-hahss
bees

bobas
boh-bahss
silly

15

Mira, Mira ...

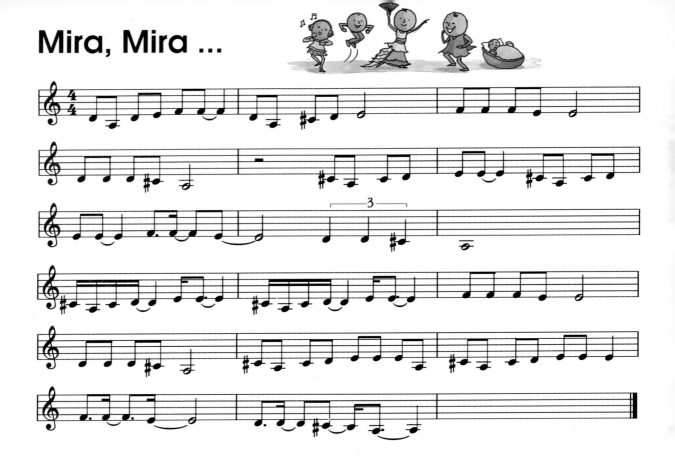

Mira, mira a Luisa,
Mira, mira a Juan.
¿Qué están haciendo?
¿Qué están haciendo?
Luisa está cantando,
Juan está saltando,
Cantando y saltando.

Mira, mira a Mamá,
Mira, mira a Papá.
¿Qué están haciendo?
¿Qué están haciendo?
Mamá está bailando,
Papá está riendo,
Bailando y riendo.

Mira, mira al bebé,
Mira, mira al bebé.
¿Qué está haciendo?
¿Qué está haciendo?
El bebé está durmiendo,
El bebé está durmiendo,
Durmiendo... durmiendo... tshh...

mira
mee-rah
look

16

cantando
cahn-tahn-doh
singing

¿Qué están haciendo?
keh ehs-tahn ah-see-en-doh
What are they doing?

saltando
sahl-tahn-doh
jumping

Luisa †
lwee-sah
Louisa

Juan †
hwahn
John

riendo
ree-en-doh
laughing

mamá †
mah-mah
Mom

bailando
by-lahn-doh
dancing

papá †
pah-pah
Dad

tshh...

tshh...

z z z z z z z

bebé †
beh-beh
baby

durmiendo
door-mee-en-doh
sleeping

17

Tengo Una Muñeca

Tengo una muñeca
Vestida de azul,
Con zapatos blancos
Y falda de tul.

La saqué a paseo
Se me enfermó,
La tengo en la cama
Con mucho dolor.

El doctor la ha visto
Y la recetó
Una bebidita
Con que se curó.

Tengo una muñeca
Vestida de azul,
Con zapatos blancos
Y falda de tul.

tengo
ten-goh
I have

muñeca †
moon-yeh-cah
doll

vestida de azul
behs-tee-dah deh ah-sool
dressed in blue

zapatos †   **blancos**
sah-pah-tohss blahn-cohss
white shoes

falda †   **de tul** †
fahl-dah deh tool
skirt of tulle

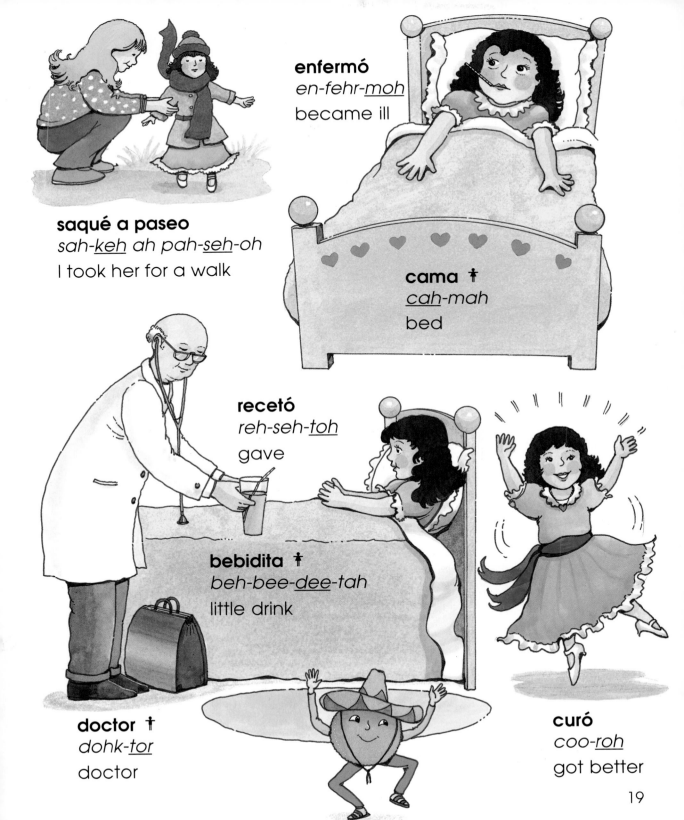

saqué a paseo
sah-keh ah pah-seh-oh
I took her for a walk

enfermó
en-fehr-moh
became ill

cama ✝
cah-mah
bed

recetó
reh-seh-toh
gave

bebidita ✝
beh-bee-dee-tah
little drink

doctor ✝
dohk-tor
doctor

curó
coo-roh
got better

19

¿Dónde Están Las Llaves?

Yo tengo un castillo
Matarile - rile - rile,
Yo tengo un castillo
Matarile - rile - rón,
Chim - pón.

¿Dónde están las llaves?
Matarile - rile - rile,
¿Dónde están las llaves?
Matarile - rile - rón,
Chim - pón.

En el fondo del mar
Matarile - rile - rile,
En el fondo del mar
Matarile - rile - rón,
Chim - pón.

¿Quién irá a buscarlas?
Matarile - rile - rile,
¿Quién irá a buscarlas?
Matarile - rile - rón,
Chim - pón.

Irá Carmencita
Matarile - rile - rile,
Irá Carmencita
Matarile - rile - rón,
Chim - pón.

¿Qué oficio le pondremos?
Matarile - rile - rile,
¿Qué oficio le pondremos?
Matarile - rile - rón,
Chim - pón.

Le pondremos Reina de España
Matarile - rile - rile,
Le pondremos Reina de España
Matarile - rile - rón,
Chim - pón.

21

¿Dónde Están Las Llaves?

yo tengo
yoh ten-goh
I have

castillo †
cahs-tee-yoh
castle

llaves †
yah-behss
keys

¿Dónde están las llaves?
dohn-deh ehs-tahn lahss yah-behss
Where are the keys?

en el fondo †   **del mar** †
en el fohn-doh del mar
at the bottom of the sea

22

¿Quién irá a buscarlas?
kee-en ee-rah ah boos-car-lahss
Who will look for them?

Carmencita ✝
car-men-see-tah
Carmencita

señora
Reina

oficio ✝
oh-fee-see-oh
title

le pondremos
leh pohn-dreh-mohss
we shall call her

Reina ✝
reh-nah
Queen

España ✝
ehs-pahn-yah
Spain

ESPAÑA

Caballito Blanco

Caballito blanco
Llévame de aquí.
Llévame a mi pueblo
Donde yo nací.

Tengo, tengo, tengo,
Tú no tienes nada.
Tengo tres ovejas
En una cabaña.

Una me da leche,
Otra me da lana,
Otra queso blanco
Para la semana.

llévame
yeh-bah-meh
take me

caballito †
cah-bah-yee-toh
little horse

blanco
blahn-coh
white

24

pueblo †
pweh-bloh
village

tengo
ten-goh
I have

nací
nah-see
born

tú no tienes nada
too noh tee-eh-nehss nah-dah
you have nothing

me
meh
me

una
oo-nah
one

leche †
leh-cheh
milk

tres
trehss
three

lana †
lah-nah
wool

otra
oh-trah
other

ovejas †
oh-beh-hahss
sheep

en
en
in

queso blanco †
keh-soh blahn-coh
cream cheese

cabaña †
cah-bahn-yah
hut

25

Cucú Cantaba La Rana

Cucú, cucú, (refrain)
Cantaba la rana,
Debajo del agua.
Pasó un caballero,
Con capa y sombrero.
Pasó una señora,
Con traje de cola.
Pasó un marinero,
Llevando romero.
Le pedí un ramito,
No me lo quiso dar.
Le cogí del brazo
Y le hice bailar.
Si el cucú te gusta
Volveré a empezar.

Cucú Cantaba La Rana

cucú
coo-coo
coocoo

cantaba
cahn-tah-bah
sang

rana †
rah-nah
frog

debajo
deh-bah-hoh
under

agua †
ah-gwah
water

sombrero †
sohm-breh-roh
hat

capa †
cah-pah
cape

caballero †
cah-bah-yeh-roh
gentleman

traje † **de cola** †
trah-heh deh coh-lah
dress with a train

señora †
sehn-yoh-rah
lady

llevando
yeh-bahn-doh
carrying

romero †
roh-meh-roh
rosemary

marinero †
mah-ree-neh-roh
sailor

ramito †
rah-mee-toh
sprig

brazo †
brah-soh
arm

volveré a empezar
bohl-beh-reh ah em-peh-sar
I shall start again

bailar
by-lar
dance

29

Ratón, Que Te Pilla El Gato

Ratón, que te pilla el gato.
Ratón, que te va a pillar.
Si no te pilla esta noche,
Mañana te pillará.

ratón †
rah-tohn
mouse

te
teh
you

gato †
gah-toh
cat

pilla
pee-yah
catch

noche †
noh-cheh
night

mañana
mahn-yah-nah
tomorrow

30

Translations

Las Cosas Que Me Gustan
The Things That I Like

I like cake,
I like coffee,
But most of all I like
Your eyes.

I like fruit,
I like tea,
But most of all I like
Your eyes.

I like bread,
I like milk,
But most of all I like
Your eyes.

Los Pollitos
The Little Chicks

The little chicks say
Cheep, cheep, cheep,
When they are hungry,
When they are cold.

Cheep, cheep, cheep, etc.

The hen looks for
Corn and wheat
And brings them food
To the nest.

Cheep, cheep, cheep, etc.

The little chicks sleep
All huddled up
Under her two wings,
Until another day.

Cheep, cheep, cheep, etc.

Pinpón
Pinpon

Pinpon is a doll
With a cardboard face.
He washes his little face
With water and with soap, with soap.

He combs his hair
With an ivory comb.
And although it pulls his hair,
He doesn't cry or make a fuss.

As he always obeys his mother,
He studies his lessons
Before he goes to bed, to bed.

And when the stars
Begin to shine,
Pinpon goes to bed.
He says his prayers and begins to dream,
To dream.

Los Colores Del Arco Iris
The Colors Of The Rainbow

What color is the apple?
It is red, red, red.

What color is the orange?
It is orange, orange, orange,

What color is the banana?
It is yellow, yellow, yellow.

What color is the ball?
It is green, green, green.

What color is the sky?
It is blue, blue, blue.

What color is the violet?
It is purple, purple, purple.

What color is the rainbow?
It is red and orange, yellow and
Green, blue and purple.

¿Quién Llama A La Ventana?
Who Is Tapping At The Window?

Tap! Tap! Tap!
Who is tapping at the window?
Trumpet,
One large elephant.

Miaow, miaow, miaow,
Two very little kittens.

Baa, baa, baa,
Three old sheep.

Cluck, cluck, cluck,
Four white hens.

Bzzz, bzzz, bzzz,
Five silly bees.

Mira, Mira...
Look, Look...

Look, look at Louisa,
Look, look at John.
What are they doing?
What are they doing?
Louisa is singing,
John is jumping,
Singing and jumping.

Look, look at Mom,
Look, look at Dad.
What are they doing?
What are they doing?
Mom is dancing,
Dad is laughing,
Dancing and laughing.

Look, look at the baby,
Look, look at the baby,
What is he doing?
What is he doing?
The baby is sleeping,
The baby is sleeping,
Sleeping... sleeping... shh.

31

Tengo Una Muñeca
I Have A Doll

I have a doll
Dressed in blue,
With white shoes
And skirt of tulle.

I took her for a walk
When she became ill,
I put her to bed
In great pain.

The doctor visited her
And gave her
A little drink
And then she got better.

I have a doll
Dressed in blue,
With white shoes
And skirt of tulle.

¿Dónde Están Las Llaves?
Where Are The Keys?

I have a little castle
Matarile - rile - rile,
I have a little castle
Matarile - rile - ron,
Chim - pon.

Where are the keys?
Matarile - rile - rile,
Where are the keys?
Matarile - rile - ron,
Chim - pon.

At the bottom of the sea
Matarile - rile - rile,
At the bottom of the sea
Matarile - rile - ron,
Chim - pon.

Who will look for them?
Matarile - rile - rile,
Who will look for them?
Matarile - rile - ron,
Chim - pon.

Carmencita will go
Matarile - rile - rile,
Carmencita will go
Matarile - rile - ron,
Chim - pon.

What shall we call her?
Matarile - rile - rile,
What shall we call her?
Matarile - rile - ron,
Chim - pon.

We shall call her the Queen of Spain
Matarile - rile - rile,
We shall call her the Queen of Spain
Matarile - rile - ron,
Chim - pon.

Caballito Blanco
Little White Horse

Little white horse
Take me away from here.
Take me back to my village
Where I was born.

I have, I have, I have,
You haven't got anything.
I have three sheep
In a hut.

One gives me milk,
The other gives me wool,
And the other gives me cream cheese
For the whole week.

Cucú Cantaba La Rana
Coocoo Sang The Frog

Coocoo, coocoo, (refrain)
Sang the frog,
Under the water.
A gentleman went by,
In a cape and hat.
A lady went by,
In a dress with a train.
A sailor went by,
Carrying rosemary.
I asked him for a little sprig,
Which he would not give me.
I took him by the arm
And he danced with me.
If you like the coocoo sound
I shall start again.

Ratón, Que Te Pilla El Gato
Mouse, Beware The Cat Will Catch You

Mouse, beware the cat will catch you.
Mouse, you're going to be caught.
If he doesn't catch you tonight,
Tomorrow he will.

With our thanks to the children who
sang these songs:
Amaya, Elisa, Flor, Guido, Rocío.

Thanks also to our Spanish consultants:
Javier Domínguez and Diana Terry.

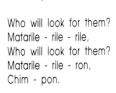